Camel's Wool and Honey

Mark 1:1–8 for children

Written by Jeffrey E. Burkart
Illustrated by Robin DeWitt

Arch® Books

Copyright © 2000 Concordia Publishing House
3558 S. Jefferson Avenue, St. Louis, MO 63118-3968
Manufactured in the United States of America

Two prophets of the Lord once wrote:
"God's messenger is nearing!
And he will pave the way for Christ
Before the Lord's appearing.

"Out of the desert you will hear
A voice of one proclaiming.
'Make straight the paths. Prepare His way!'
The voice will be exclaiming!"

And sure enough, a man named John
Stood in the desert preaching.
The city and the country folk
Went there to hear his teaching.

He wore a coat of camel's hair,
And though it seems quite funny,
For dinner he ate jumping bugs
Washed down with lots of honey.

John preached repentance and baptized
All those who came confessing
That they were sorry for their sins
And were in need of blessing.

The people went to be baptized
In Jordan River's water.
And every person who was washed
Was God's own son and daughter.

John said, "Praise be to God our Lord;
His people God's redeeming.
And those who sit in darkness now
Will find God's light is beaming.

"The light of God will point the way
To peace and to salvation!
This Good News that I'm speaking of
Is meant for every nation.

"The Lord is coming soon!" John said.
"Make straight the crooked highways!
Repent *now*, for the *Promised One*
Will walk these earthly byways!"

"Soon after me Someone will come
All powerful and caring.
And I'm unworthy to untie
The sandals *He'll* be wearing.

"I baptize you with water now,
But *He* will surely shower
Each one of you with His good gift—
The Holy Spirit's power."

Now Jesus our Messiah's come!
Good News to you He's preaching.
He will enfold you in His love;
With open arms He's reaching.

His arms were open to us all
When on the cross extended,
Our Lord and Savior gave His life,
And everything was mended.

He took away our sins that day;
With His own life He bought us.
He rose up from the grave, and in
His loving arms He caught us.

In loving arms He'll bear us up
And grant to us salvation.
Do not be silent. Spread God's Word
Through every land and nation.

With joy and thanks give praise to God—
The Father, Son, and Spirit.
And just like John the Baptist tell
Good News to all who'll hear it.

Dear Parents:

Camel's hair and honey—what an existence! John the Baptist lived in the wilderness, taking his food and clothing from his surroundings. Camel's hair was the traditional garb of Old Testament prophets, especially Elijah (see 2 Kings 1:8). John denied self-indulgence for the sake of his prophetic message—"Repent and be baptized!"

John was a voice in the wilderness, imploring people to turn away from their sin and back to God (see Psalm 51:10). John's words proclaimed that the Messiah was coming, one mightier than he, through whom God would work His plan for salvation.

You and your child can be voices in the wilderness too. You can proclaim the message that the Messiah *has* come. Is there someone you or your child know who needs to hear that God sent His Son to take our sins to the cross and proclaim victory through His resurrection? Tell them the Good News today!

The Editor